We Are Magical Beings

A Healing Guide for Earthlings

Paola Collazos, LMT

BALBOA.
PRESS

A DIVISION OF HAY HOUSE

Balboa Press books may be ordered through
booksellers or by contacting:

Balboa Press
A Division of Hay House
1663 Liberty Drive
Bloomington, IN 47403
www.balboapress.com
1 (877) 407-4847

Because of the dynamic nature of the Internet, any web
addresses or links contained in this book may have changed
since publication and may no longer be valid. The views
expressed in this work are solely those of the author and do
not necessarily reflect the views of the publisher, and the
publisher hereby disclaims any responsibility for them.

The author of this book does not dispense medical advice or prescribe
the use of any technique as a form of treatment for physical,
emotional, or medical problems without the advice of a physician,
either directly or indirectly. The intent of the author is only to offer
information of a general nature to help you in your quest for emotional
and spiritual well-being. In the event you use any of the information
in this book for yourself, which is your constitutional right, the
author and the publisher assume no responsibility for your actions.

Any people depicted in stock imagery provided by Thinkstock are
models, and such images are being used for illustrative purposes only.
Certain stock imagery © Thinkstock.

Print information available on the last page.

ISBN: 978-1-5043-8718-7 (sc)
ISBN: 978-1-5043-8720-0 (hc)
ISBN: 978-1-5043-8719-4 (e)

Library of Congress Control Number: 2017913687

Balboa Press rev. date: 10/19/2017

Contents

The words that follow are dedicated to time, body, spirit, and mind, for without them, all experiences, good or bad, would not be lovely memories. Special praise to love, expression, connections, forgiveness—to life itself, to pain, to joy, and even to the mundane.

Introduction

Life is a series of moments, some difficult and others beautiful. Though we all experience variations of pain and ease, both physical and emotional, throughout our lives, I believe that we can all obtain health, peace and happiness. My intention is to briefly share my story because it is through my own pain and truth that I found healing.

I have been an energy work practitioner, licensed massage therapist, spirit coach, and Reiki practitioner for over ten years, eventually becoming a Reiki master. Through this line of work, I have encountered many beautiful beings and have helped them deal with their physical or emotional pain through bodywork, meditation, and energy-focused techniques. The first part of this book is an unfolding of my early life experiences and the events that led to my healing. The second part is a simplified description on health from an energetic perspective and how to keep your own energy in alignment. Aside from bodywork, I have also been working with the families of special needs children, guiding them through the changes that come with having a special-needs child. In my spare time as a volunteer, I have led various community art programs.

My parents met in New York, specifically in Corona, Queens, in the late 1970s. Corona was a world in itself, home to immigrants trying to find a different life for themselves. My mother and grandmother found a home amongst a community of people from all over Latin America.

My mother and grandmother arrived in the United States from Argentina in 1978, right in the middle of Jorge Rafael Videla's military rule that resulted in thirty thousand disappearances. I remember watching my grandmother as she talked about the lachrymatory agents that were at times launched during public gatherings in order to control young protestors. Her large fingers crossed and uncrossed nervously on her lap. Her gaze shifted as she changed her dialogue to that one evening she had to pull my teenage mother out of a military truck because the coffee shop she frequented had been raided. She had heard the news from a neighbor who had come to their door. Telling the story with a tinge of excitement, she explained how she hopped out of bed with her nightgown still on and gave those military bastards a piece of her mind, demanding that they release her daughter. My grandma Celia always felt that if she had stayed in Argentina, my mother, who was about seventeen, would have definitely gotten into trouble. Trouble meant torture or death during those times. The exact details of why she had actually come to the United States are still unclear because my grandmother had not been happy in her marriage. Perhaps her arrival was a culmination of all of these factors. Either way, she made it here, an orphan without a career and who did not speak English.

To provide for herself and my mother, she got a job at a bar. Celia was a vivacious woman who quickly adapted to her surroundings and learned how to survive in New York City. Everyone loved her. On one occasion, one of her customers gave her a little bag of cocaine as a gift. Yes, cocaine was being given away like candy at the time. Instead of consuming it, she sold it later to someone else from the bar. This marked the beginning of a new and profitable way for her to make a living.

It was through this new means to an end that my mother eventually crossed paths with my father, who was from Colombia and also involved in illegal activities. My father was out of our lives quickly, but to his defense—or better yet, to my own sanity—Colombia during those times was struggling through their own complicated wars between the Colombian government, paramilitary groups, guerrillas, and dangerous drug cartels. No one knows why he chose the life he did.

I was born in Astoria, Queens, on January 30, 1980, a decade that would soon suffer economic crises, drug trafficking–related atrocities, and eventually a pandemic that not only took millions but also brought to surface hate, fear, and ignorance. I was lucky that I was spared from learning hate. My grandmother had many friends from all walks of life and preferences. Growing up, my life was an eternal example of how one should never judge others. From the exuberant Francisco, who loved makeup and loathed vaginas, to the beautiful Dina, who had three kids and supported them through prostitution, my grandmother knew them all:

the criminals, misfits, the nonconformists, and beyond.

One of the things I always say, and this is coming from my own perfect recollection of the things that happened, is that kids feel and see everything. They are wiser than given credit for, and though they may not be able to explain things or put things into context, they are aware. Only when they are older and have enough information are they able to put the pieces of their pasts together.

For me, it was not about the drugs that were being sold out of our apartment. That was happening in between tender moments with my grandmother. It was completely natural for our play to be interrupted by the doorbell. I knew he or she was there for the white powder, as I had labeled it in my little thoughts. I would hear her engage in chitchat about how things were going for each of them. Her customers were people with lives and families. They were nice to me, sometimes even embracing me and lifting me up to hug me.

Of course, she tried to be discreet about everything, but I felt something was happening. I felt the secrecy. I would see her weighing and bagging the coke, even though she would tell me to stay out of the kitchen. I knew people were coming for it. Even though I was a little kid, I understood the exchange. That's why I always say not to take your little ones for granted. They are aware and are wiser than you think.

While my mother worked her regular real estate agent job, my grandmother cooked for me and gave me love, playing along with whatever silly games I invented. I never went hungry and always had a modest roof over my head. We were not living in extravagance as you may imagine. We lived in a one-bedroom apartment. My grandmother was careful about how she did things and took pride in the face that her clients were professionals, such as lawyers, chefs, and/or businessmen. She would sell just enough for the necessities.

I was unaware of pain during my childhood. I was experiencing but not fully comprehending. Pain was something that emerged later. When I was four years old, I started sleepwalking and interacting with fairies. They would wake me up in the middle of the night and take me to the window. I remember feeling the long mauve curtains with my fingers. They were heavy and soft. I would see the fairies upon the folds of the curtains. They were not like one may imagine a fairy to be. They were like sparks of light. Their voices were soft. They would tell me that if I rubbed my eyes with the palm of my hands firmly for a few seconds, I would find darkness and eventually I would be able to see them wherever I was.

As I got older, I realized that they had arrived during the time I was being sexually abused. The abuse went on for about two years by a man who was a family member through marriage. During those times, I followed their advice on how to disconnect by rubbing my eyes. As if that were not enough, I experienced two more separate instances of sexual abuse soon after the first incident became known—one from a friend's grandfather and the other from a friend's father, all before my first dance after kindergarten graduation.

I was about six years old when my grandmother was arrested for the first time for selling cocaine to an undercover cop. She was released on bail, and we fled the United States to Puerto Rico with the help of her well-connected friends. They knew how to get her a new identity.

This, of course, meant a new social security number and name. I lived with my grandmother on the beautiful island, whereas my mother stayed behind working. During the time with my fugitive grandmother, I was enrolled in all sorts of extracurricular activities in an effort to distract me from being away from my mother, whom I missed terribly. My grandmother would spend every night teaching me how to read and write Spanish so that I would not be left back at school. She argued with the school administration to give me a chance, and it worked. They did not leave me back, and I was able to sit in class with kids of my own age.

At age six, and for years to come, I became Celia's only friend. She would tell me stories about her life as an orphan, how she saw her mother die giving herself an abortion with a hanger, how she used to sneak around with her lovers, and how to weigh cocaine, just in case I ever had to. Of course, she reiterated to me that I should find a decent job when I was older and how being bilingual would surely give me a heads up. My childhood was heavy. I don't think my grandmother meant any harm. She didn't know any better, and believe me that this way of thinking helped me heal. Caregivers do not know it all. They just do what is familiar. They do what they have learned. My grandmother was an orphan. The only thing she knew was how to survive, and inside of her was the terrible feeling of abandonment.

After a few years, we were eventually reunited with my mother in New York. Shortly after our return, I became sick with ITP, a blood disease that lasted a year. That year was defined by weekly visits to the hospital for blood work and eventually for transfusions. My grandmother embraced her new identity and continued her old working practices consistently and without any problems for exactly eleven years, until her second arrest. My life during those years was colorful, ranging from your typical teenage growing pains to heavier issues like drug and alcohol abuse and promiscuity.

My pain surfaced when I was eighteen years old. The trigger was my grandmother being arrested for the second time. There are no words to describe how painful it was for me to know that she was behind bars. Suddenly, a montage of memories rolled through my mind. I recalled how we used to have picnics in Flushing Meadow

Park, how she used to sing to me, how she made me fried eggs with fries, and how she cuddled with me when I was scared.

I remember one day clearly. I was working for the Department of Mental Health as a college intern when my mother called to tell me that my grandmother had been arrested. This time it was not for dealing but because the after-hours bar she frequented had been raided. What my sweet little grandmother was doing there in the first place was indeed reckless, but it's quite comical looking at it now. Though she revealed her sweet side to me, she had a wild and destructive side. More than a grandmother, she was a complex human being. The cops had arrested everyone, and when fingerprinted, they pulled up her file from eleven years earlier. She managed to flee the country yet again, spending the rest of her days with the husband she had abandoned years ago in Argentina. She passed away years later. I never knew her real age.

That's my story, as briefly as I can tell it. Still, with all of that, I believe in inner peace. We are magical beings who have the capacity to heal ourselves. I can say that because I did it. All people have their own pain. My story is neither more painful nor less than yours. That's the beauty of pain. It connects us as humans.

Chapter 1

The Body, Your Super Vehicle

By the age of seven, I had already experienced feelings of loneliness, abandonment, and sexual abuse. In addition, I had also lived through the sudden displacement and fear that came with having to leave the country with my grandmother. Today I can say that nothing has brought me more inner peace and understanding than studying the human body—not only its anatomy and physiology but also understanding it from an energetic perspective.

When I was a little kid, in the midst of everything, I would bombard my mother with questions about why we were here on this planet and how objects got their names. "Why is a cup called a cup, as opposed to a plate?" It's funny that this question truly perplexed me at age five. Who decided? Who was the *namer* of all objects? I would also ask her if God was telling the angels stories about us up there, surrounded by clouds. Then I would imagine him sitting on a puffy cloud with a giant golden book on his lap, surrounded by angels, telling them the story of us, the humans.

I remember always being connected to something bigger, even during my time in Puerto Rico, when everything seemed to be falling apart. While my grandmother slept endless hours in her state of depression and guilt, I used to pretend that I was a fairy princess who had the power to stir magic upon the world. I would peek out of my bedroom's unstable little balcony, with a view of the luminous green ocean, lift my arms up, and with the palms of my hands, I would send magic out into the world. I would do this and play other imaginary games, keeping myself busy for hours, patiently waiting for my grandmother to embrace me with the attention that I so urgently craved and missed. I missed the way she used to be, but I didn't fully comprehend what had happened.

I've always had this overwhelming sensibility, always trying to understand human experiences outside of myself, genuinely caring for others. Today when I see people's struggles, all I want to say is, "Stop those horrible thoughts. You are incased in an impermeable breathing structure that pumps blood just for you! How amazing is it that we can see the world's colors?"

My mother once told me that I had once reprimanded her for making fun of a celebrity couple because she had said that the woman was too pretty for the man she had married. At age five, I told my mother that beauty is on the inside. As a kid, I was perhaps the light to their chaos.

When I was thirteen, I enrolled myself in religious instruction classes, hoping to find some kind of answer for any of the events that had transpired in my life thus far. Religion was never enforced in our family, so my mother went along with my curiosity to learn. My mother was a bit of a rebellious woman who loved to draw and always encouraged me to do what I felt was right. She was perfect for the job of being my mother because she never stopped me from believing in extraordinary things. I attended the classes for a few weeks but did not find what I was looking for.

Today I don't even remember much about my experience with the religion classes except for the heaviness of the room, the smell of the frankincense, and hearing the restrictions. It was a definite change from what I was used to at home. I rejected religion with full force. I suppose that my initial reason for seeking religion was that I wanted to understand my inner self more, my spirit and my thought process. As strange as it may sound to some, I wanted to understand who the thinker inside of me was.

That same year, my sister was born. My mother had fallen in love yet again with a man who was involved in illegal activities, which of course infuriated me and caused me to rebel. Sometime after that, my mother left the state with him and my baby sister, leaving me yet again with my grandmother, who was not an enforcer of rules. During that time, I was coming and going as I saw fit. Despite my sometimes destructive behavior during that time, I managed to keep up with high school and graduate. My mother eventually returned, exhausted by a man who was abusive.

I started college as a liberal arts student, and a metaphysics professor greatly inspired me. He taught us a lesson on the idea of the changing self. I had never heard this train of thought before: "The you of the past is no longer the same as the you in the present. So are you still you?"

This question, though I had not asked it in the same way prior to the class, was the core of my wonder. I decided to major in philosophy with a minor in comparative religion. As far as religion, it was because I was fascinated by the similarities between religions as opposed to the differences and the histories behind them. At the core of it, for me, the answer was simple: we are all human beings. We all needed to believe in something, to have a purpose, to ease our fears about death, and to feel a sense of belonging. Without this basic ease, we would just be a bunch of breathing skin and bones on a floating speck of rock in the middle of an infinite expanding universe.

I know now that my fascination with religion and philosophy was also a result of the events I had experienced. As I got older, it became extremely difficult for me to understand and justify the paths my caregivers had chosen. In a sense, it was like living a double life. I could never fully express who I was to anyone, and if I did, I risked being judged. I didn't want to feel victimized or put my mother and grandmother in jeopardy. I didn't want that then or now. As I got older, I could no longer ignore the social ramifications of what was going on around me. These feelings definitely impacted my identity.

My major changed because I did not find what I was looking for in endless theories that tangled and complicated the meaning of life. It changed because everything around me changed. I was about eighteen, and my grandmother had gotten arrested for the second time. Not even for dealing. She had gotten arrested for being in an after-hours establishment that was raided. I got the call from my mother at work. "They pulled her file from eleven years ago," my mother said. Just like that, life took my dearest love away in the worst possible manner. How could I continue to live knowing that my grandmother would be locked away in prison, this time perhaps until the end of her days?

I had been in search for the meaning of life for as long as I can remember. For me, the meaning of life had to be beautiful, it had to feel good, and it had to be easy for everyone to understand. But I could not understand life at that moment. Nothing felt good. The sexual abuse that I had pushed aside began to haunt me in my dreams.

You see, I always had recollections of the thing that happened, but not to the full extent. All the memories came pouring back, clear memories of the time in the bedroom, the time in the bathroom, in the car, on the couch, the way he lured me. I could not shake the feeling of dirtiness. I felt like an immobile bag of flesh and bones. I was empty and filled the void with cigarettes, sex, alcohol, and eventually drugs.

A good friend of mine had noticed that my world was falling apart and suggested I go for a Reiki healing session. Reiki is a form of energy work in which practitioners set their hands upon energy centers in the body to promote energetic balance. Practitioners do not use their own energy to do this. In other words, they are not giving you their energy. They work with the receiver's own energy systems to promote wellness. They do not do anything that your own body is not ready for. This is the case for all forms of energy work. My friend had explained that I should trust her and go for a session because she could not describe what she had felt during her session. However, she was sure that I would feel better.

I agreed to go. The day of the session, I was

nervous and a little scared because I had no clue what I was getting into. The practitioner led me to an office. She sat behind a desk that was completely cluttered with paper and books, a wooden bookshelf behind her, and a huge window toward the side. The light of the sun poured in toward us. She asked me some questions and proceeded with the session. She instructed me to get on the table facing up, and she placed her hands on my feet, eventually making her way up my chakras (energy centers along the midline of the body). Her hands did not touch me directly. They hovered over the centers, and I felt warmth coming from her hands.

A few minutes into it, she started to cry. She said she saw and felt a lot of pain in me. Of course, this completely freaked me out. I believed she was putting on an act. I left as soon as I was able and cursed out my friend for sending me to a crazy woman who only wanted my money! But the truth was that I was in a lot of pain at the time. Years later, I came to realize that people fear things they do not understand, so they reject and ignore them. I was simply not ready to face it in that moment, and I didn't yet understand that some people are more able to perceive energy than others are. She probably shouldn't have cried in front of me, but life unfolds perfectly and sometimes you need to trust that unfolding.

I randomly stumbled upon Reiki again not too long after that first encounter. I was looking at crystals that were being sold in an outdoor market. The woman selling them invited me to a Reiki class. I shared my experience with her, and she explained that the class would teach me how Reiki works and also how to use Reiki to heal others. I paid more attention to her because it felt like a sign to me. Reiki was being offered to me again. *How curious*, I had thought. This time it was introduced in a different context and along with crystal healing, which I was much more comfortable with.

As a kid I'd learned about crystals and their healing properties from a friend's mom. I had spent a lot of time at their house while my caregivers were busy trying to survive. Seeing my friend's mother Emmie explore various religions and ways of thinking about life throughout the years shaped me. Without knowing it, she taught me that it was okay to search for what feels right, no matter what people think. Emmie was a free spirit who lit incense and talked about crystals and Egyptian history. During those times, she suddenly converted to Muslim, hijab and all. I was there to witness the reactions of the people who lived in our building and how she stood so proudly, no matter what they said behind her back. She was trying to find her faith and her position in her world. She taught me that it is okay to question and not accept things blindly—that people can change and no one can tell you how to get to your inner self and how to connect with your higher power.

Therefore, with Emmie in my thoughts, I went to the Reiki class one week later, feeling a little skeptical but going along with the signs. The class was held in the Reiki master's home. There were about five of us present for the class, which explained that Reiki is a healing art in which practitioners place their hands on specific energy centers to promote balance and activate the receiver's own natural healing.

We learned about chakra centers, what they were and where they are located in the body. We also learned the Reiki symbols, which we were supposed to visualize simultaneously with our minds while hovering over each chakra with our hands when working with our own chakras or eventually with clients. We discovered that once we learned the hand placements, symbols, and energy centers, we can chose to be attuned to be first-degree Reiki practitioners. The purpose of the first attunement is to connect the students to their inner selves, raise their energy levels, and open them up to infinite universal life energy. It was suggested that after the first attunement, the students should focus on doing Reiki on themselves. The second attunement connects the student more deeply to universal energy, making them more able to work on others and do distance healing. It promoted a deeper emotional healing. The third attunement, or the master level, should be done after the practitioner has had a lot of experience, for at this level, one can now attune and teach others.

After my first attunement, which I received that same day, I was convinced this was what I had always been looking for. To pass the attunement, the master stood over me. I sat down on a straight-backed chair, pressing my palms together in front of my chest. I had my eyes closed, but I peeked slightly, receiving glimpses of his warm hands waving symbols all around me. He did this for some time. I then felt him blow breath into my crown chakra and on my back, near my solar plexus. As he was blowing, I felt what can only be described as a euphoric embrace, and then shortly after, I wanted to cry and laugh at the same time. I was no longer peeking to see what was going on. I felt as though something was carrying me. I knew it was universal life force, and I trusted the attunement. He then opened my hands and traced a symbol on my palm, followed by three taps. He did this four times. He was opening my hand chakras.

The evening had gone by too quickly, but I was filled with love and purpose. I started the commute back home. It was the first time I had gone to New Jersey on the train. The streets were quiet, and everything felt lighter. I was definitely different, but the weeks that followed solidified this difference. For one, the next day my body started to detox naturally. No matter how many deodorants I tried that week, they did not work. I stunk no matter what I used. My body's chemistry seemed to be changing. I also stopped enjoying the taste of meat. This was particularly striking for me because I grew up in an Argentinean household and eating meat was part of our culture. Aside from that, I wasn't familiar with the concept of vegetarianism or even animal activism at the time. I was an eighteen-year-old girl from Queens, New York, with a mediocre public school education. How could it be that such core preferences would change so abruptly in a matter of days? I knew it was the attunement. I now believed in a higher power, or what some call God.

My view of the world changed, and I began to feel and see energy in others and in myself. I spent the next year reading about energy and doing Reiki on myself. I was fascinated by the changes in me. I learned that in order to be able to pass attunements as a master, one must be able to control the breath and have the ability to hold the Hui Yin position for long periods. The Hui Yin, I discovered, is the beginning of a meridian known as Conception Vessel, or CV 1, located at the perineum (area between the anus and genitals). Meridians are energy pathways typically used in Chinese medicine or acupuncture. Holding the position means that one is able to allow this energy to complete a figure eight–shaped circuit between the Conception

Vessel and Governing Vessel, which is also a meridian. This is called the microcosmic orbit, but I call it activating the orbit. (I talk more about it later in this book.) The master is able to attune the student by tapping into this energy and moving the student's energy. It is a transfer from master to student. The attunement process opens the crown, heart and palm chakras. The attunement is a profound spiritual experience. Reiki is a profound spiritual experience that is difficult to describe in words. Sometimes things are too big to be described in words but can be felt. This is Reiki.

For me, this energy was the truth I was seeking. It was not in texts or in organized religion. It was an energy that I could actually feel, and it flowed in everything. It was source. I called it the hum because it was how source sounded to me. Most importantly, I felt I had physical evidence of source. We are magical beings, and it is possible to heal ourselves. If I did it, anyone can.

After my first attunement, I spent a lot of time working on my own chakras. I was profoundly connected with source, communicating with her through verses that came to me effortlessly. I followed her signs. I also acquainted myself with my spirit guides that came to me during my own healings.

I did my second attunement about a year after the first. As I've mentioned, after the second attunement, one can start to work on others and do distance healing. After doing sessions on several people, I felt the need to understand the body in more depth. The first time I realized this was during a Reiki session I was giving. I had been working on a particular area for some time, and I felt what I could only explain as heaviness or the sense of wanting to cry. I remembered my first experience with the woman who had cried after giving me a session, and I understood her. It was clear now. Of course, I held back my tears because I remembered how uncomfortable that had once made me. Instead, I waited until after the session. I asked the receiver if she had anything going on in the area where I had felt the feeling of crying. She confirmed that she had injured her back and had a herniated disk. I was able to perceive her area of discomfort without knowing that information prior to the session. That was amazing to me. I believed in my abilities; however, I also knew the importance of developing better language in order to explain energy without having it sound like mumbo jumbo.

I quickly decided to go to massage therapy school. I thought this was perfect because I would be able to continue to use my hands while also learning more about the human body. I went to the Swedish institute in New York, where they provided an extensive curriculum. There I learned both Eastern and Western approaches and techniques for working with the body. I gravitated more toward Eastern modalities and have been studying the body's subtle energies ever since. These modalities included shiatsu, which is a Japanese form of bodywork in which the practitioner works with clients' meridians in order to balance their energy. The practitioner will use fingers, palms, elbows, or knees to promote balance gently upon the needed meridian. I also enjoy using CranioSacral Therapy techniques. CST is a form of bodywork that involves very light touch upon certain points on the cranium and sacrum. It is through these points that a practitioner is able to detect the rhythm of the cerebrospinal fluid, which can relieve pain and trauma. I continued to do Reiki and later completed a foundations course in energy medicine. Energy medicine combined all the energy-moving approaches I had already learned into one effective way of healing and talking about the body. It essentially glued everything together for me.

To say it simply, the human body is an amazing and almost magical structure. Only a very wise force could have created its design. The force that has created everything in nature. The force that is inside all of us.

The brain is constantly busy sending electrical impulses via the spine in order to keep the body moving you through the world. Imagine if we actually had to think about digesting that bacon cheeseburger we scarfed that day. That would mean something else for us to remember to do in our already busy lives. We feel it happening, but the stomach, if healthy, does what it needs to do. We open our eyes and simply see, we breathe, and we smell. You don't have to flick a switch in order to do these things. The mind and body are constantly busy just living. If that isn't enough to make us believe that we are extraordinary beings, I don't know what is.

The brain faithfully processes and delivers information via an intricate system that sends electrical impulses up and down the spine. Nature's motherboard! All day it does this, despite all the extra everyday stressors of modern life, both physical and emotional.

Of course, our bodies are eventually beaten up and worn as time passes. When people say that stress is the root of all illness, they are not kidding. Stress is anything that bothers you. It does not matter if it is a high level or low-level stressor. Your body does not really differentiate. Further still, we tend to push our past experiences in the background, hidden away, hoping that those things that we perceived as bad in the past do not pop up again.

The brain does not help either, because in an effort to protect us, it can automatically block traumatic events. This happened to me; I repressed the details of my sexual abuse until I was about eighteen. The concept of repressed memories is not a new concept. Sigmund Freud introduced it in the late 1800s. He proposed that the brain can automatically block trauma without the person intending to block it. This concept is controversial, for he did not gather this information from scientific studies. He gathered it from his patients. In a more recent study conducted at Stanford University and the University of Oregon, it has been shown that a biological mechanism exists in the human brain, blocking unwanted memories.

We tend not to follow our dreams and our hearts, and that can eventually cause havoc as well. Over time, our bodies start to break down due to stress, toxins in the environment, and negative thinking habits that crush the life and health out of us. The good news is that once you can understand this, once you can gain some control over your body and your thoughts, your super vehicle, you will be healthier and happier.

Chapter 2

Energy

We are energy! Energy is always flowing through us and around us. It is in everything we encounter in our lives. What we think, say, do, and eat matters to our well-being and to the world. If someone told me I was beautiful, I'd bashfully try to hide it by saying, "Oh, stop it!" However, it would most definitely ignite happiness within me and set me off on a good day. On the other hand, if I ate something greasy on the go and someone pushed into me and called me ugly, that would be enough for me to not be so nice to the next person I saw.

The body is a wise self-healing structure. Each of its organs and systems are designed to keep us going so that we can live, be happy, and find the purpose of our lives. We are inside nature's vehicle, rolling through life experience, and nothing is more inspiring than that!

In addition to our organs, limbs, blood, and systems, there are other more subtle systems that are also extremely important to us as multidimensional energetic beings. These energetic systems are meridians, chakras, and the aura. It is uncommon to hear about these systems unless you practice yoga or have had an acupuncture treatment or other form of energy work. Though we do not often hear about these other systems when we go see the doctor or read about them in conventional health textbooks, these systems have been discussed and studied for centuries, and it is time we pay more attention to them, for they play crucial roles in our well-being.

Meridians

Meridians are energetic channels that exist in the body. They deliver energy to organs and physiological systems. Each of our organs has a meridian. There are fourteen meridians in the body, two of which do not pertain to organs. These two are called Governing Vessel and Conception Vessel. GV runs from the base of the spine to the top of the head, over and down between the eyebrows, ending at the top of the center of the lip. CV runs straight up the front of the body, from the perineum to the top of the head, connecting at the bottom of the lip. GV and CV are important suppliers of energy to all the other meridians. It is also the energy I discussed previously, when explaining the attunement for Reiki. The reason yoga and acupuncture can be so beneficial is because they are directly tapping into all of these systems by stretching and creating space for the meridian to flow (yoga) and/or by placing a needle in meridian points (acupuncture) to disperse blocked energy or control excess energy.

Chakras

Chakras are spiraling energy centers that nourish the meridians, organs, and pretty much anything near the specific chakra. Blocked chakras can cause disease. There are seven chakras in the body.

Chakra Themes

Root chakra – The root chakra center's theme is associated with the natural instinct to procreate, not only in the sense of giving life but also with the desire to live. It provides the security one needs to move forward in life. It is your survival instincts and is of course linked with sexual urges. In addition, it stores both negative and positive information about your connection with others. When root chakra is blocked, one can feel ungrounded or disconnected. It is located on the base of the spine.

Womb chakra – Contains information on creativity and our childlike wonder for life. It is trusting and flowing. Womb chakra can be the source of healing abilities. It is also associated with sexuality. It is located below the belly button.

Solar plexus – Associated with logic, organization, ego, identity, and power. When out of balance, one can feel anxious, guilt, paranoia, and/or anger. It stores information on who we are in the world, how people view us, and/or what we want from life. Solar plexus also fuels more organs than any other chakra. These organs are the liver, gallbladder, spleen, pancreas, stomach, kidneys, and adrenals. The solar plexus is located between the sternum and above the belly button.

Heart chakra – Seeks connection; embraces love for others and love for oneself. When unbalanced, it can lead to overidentifying with someone else's pain or cause one to get involved in codependent behaviors. It is located below the clavicle.

Throat chakra – The center for expression and communication. It helps us sense truth in what we are saying or hearing. It is located above the throat.

Third-eye chakra – Attracts information from the external and integrates it into thoughts. It is an area of sensory perception, abstract ideas, and intuition. It is located between the eyebrows.

Crown chakra – The area of spiritual connection, meditation, or universal wisdom. It is located at the very top of the head. It is curious that in many religions, it is common to have this area covered.

Aura

The aura is the body's outer electric magnetic field. It is oval shaped and has seven layers. It exists to protect the body from damaging energies, and it helps to bring in healthier ones to the body. It also contains information about your emotional and physical state. You can think of it as your ultimate super Brita force field. If the filter is new, it will provide fresh water. If not, it will give you murky water. Physical, emotional, and spiritual health rely on a healthy aura. Some people are able to see auras around the physical body. I can also perceive the auras on others and believe anyone can see it with practice. The aura can be bright or dark, with many other colors in between.

The information that I provide about the energy systems in the body is based on my extensive studies, training in bodywork from accredited schools, and readings about the subject. Some books that expand on the above subjects are *Essential Reiki*, by Diane Stein; *Energy Ecstasy and Your Seven Vital Chakras*, by Bernard Gunther; Qigong: A Legacy in Chinese Healing, by Dean Y. Deng MD and Enid

Ballin; *Between Heaven and Earth,* by Harriet Beinfield, L.Ac., and Efrem Korngold, L.Ac., OMD; and *Energy Medicine,* by Donna Eden and David Feinstein, PhD.

I'd like to point out that there is overlap in all these practices and modalities. In Reiki, for example, a practitioner is tapping into the chakras and meridians in order to balance energy. You can go for a session in order to have someone do it for you or you can work on yourself. The goal of tai chi and qigong is to create balance between the same basic energy systems. Tai chi is a form of meditation in motion practiced in Chinese traditions, and qigong is a form of health system integrating breath, intention, and postures meant to align life force energy. In qigong, for example, they work mostly with Conception and Governing vessels. In Shiatsu, practitioners also work with meridians by pushing on the client's channels with their thumbs or body weight. In CranioSacral therapy, they are working with the brain and spine in order to find the still point inside the nervous system fluid or CSF (cerebrospinal fluid). These modalities are like different routes to the same purpose: alignment. The good news is that you can work on all of these systems yourself.

1. If you are unable to take a class or session, take the time to stretch your back, torso, and limbs. Any stretching that you can incorporate into your everyday routine will activate movement within some aspect of the meridian system. Make circles with your feet, neck, and wrists. Move all major joints.

2. Soak your feet and rub your hands, head, and face. Most meridians either end or start on the hands, face, or feet. When rubbing your hands and feet, rub away from the body as if you are pulling the energy out.

3. Wash your face with intention. I usually take a cotton ball and soak it with witch hazel toner. I also add a few drops of essential oils to the witch hazel bottle. Lavender, patchouli, and rose are good scents for me, but choose whatever scent you like best. Gently start cleaning your forehead side to side. At the end of your eyebrows near the temples, you will feel a

slight indent. Press your fingers and make little circles on it. This point is wonderful for stress reduction. Then move between the eyebrows. This area is loaded with plenty of exploratory potential because it is where the third eye chakra rests. It is a place where you can activate intuition and sensory perception. Take your time there. Then move to the high point of your cheekbones and press firmly there. It is a good place to activate digestion, metabolism, and grounding because it is on the stomach meridian. From the cheekbones, move to the nasal ala (wing of the nose) and press the edge of it. Then head midpoint on the eyebrows, hold and pull up. This point is good for headaches, and it lies along the gallbladder meridian. By pressing on the edge of the nasal ala, you are activating the large intestine meridian, which is good for letting things go.

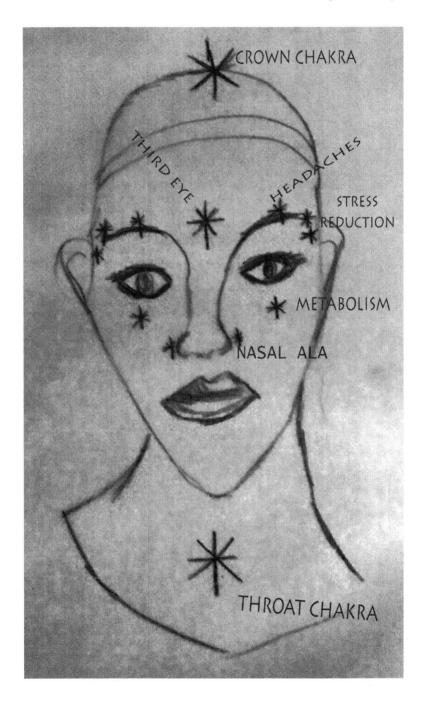

Working on your own chakras is helpful because each center is influencing any organ, ligament, or bone around it. In addition, chakras contain information on past experiences. It is a spiraling energy that when blocked can create illness or feelings that prevent one from moving forward. When you work on your meridians, you are not only tapping into energy pathways that relate to a specific organ; you are also taking the time to do something for yourself. The very action of intending to do something for yourself is beneficial to your well-being.

1. Close your eyes and relax your eyelids. Rest your hands on each chakra, warming the area, starting with the root chakra and ending at the crown chakra. Stay in the chakra as long as you feel necessary. Some chakras may require more time than others do. Trust yourself that you will know when to move. You can directly place your hands on the center or hover over the area a few inches away from it. Pay attention to any feelings, colors, thoughts, or memories that come up during your time with a chakra. Notice

but do not judge—then let it go. Remember to go back to the chakra theme section above to make the exercise more relative.

2. Draw the infinity symbol with your hands over the chakra. This is the infinity symbol:

   ∞ (it is a figure eight.)

3. You can draw the infinity symbol between anything that you wish to pacify. For example, you can imagine a person or memory that you have issues with and visualize the infinity symbol between you and that person or event. This is beneficial because sometimes our memories continue to burden us in the present. By intending to pacify the memory, you are energetically letting go of it or starting to make peace with it. We cannot move forward if the weight of negative memories continues to haunt us.

4. Placing a crystal on a chakra can absorb negative energies. Quartz or rose quartz are good ones to start with. Before and after using any crystals, wash them with water and place them under the sun for a few hours. You can also cleanse the center

by making counterclockwise motions over it with your hands. You can also place your hands on it and visualize with your mind a slow-moving spiral over it. In Reiki, a practitioner will visualize the *Cho Ku Rei*, a spiral-looking image that means *Place the power of the universe here*, during healing sessions. You can retrieve Reiki symbols online or in the book *Essential Reiki*, by Diane Stein, if you have an interest. I do not wish to display the symbols in this book due to the symbols' sacred nature. It is a personal preference.

5. You can also visualize colors or images. When visualizing colors, you can start with using white because of its association with purity. If other colors come up, simply allow them to come. I would like to stress that this exercise is about developing a personal dialogue between you and the center. Any color that comes to your head for a particular area is of benefit. When using images, you can use things like a fresh spring, a waterfall, or meadows. Use images that are positive and have meaning for you. When I was working on my root

chakra to heal from sexual abuse, I would visualize a warm waterfall pouring over it. I would also visualize fairies or angels doing the pouring. Remember to always refer back to the chakra themes. For example, let's say you are shy and want to work on that issue. You can perhaps work on solar plexus and throat chakras by using any of the techniques I describe. Choose the one that feels best for you.

Working with your aura is helpful because it is your outer energy field. It is protecting all your other energy systems. It allows you to move happily through life, protecting you from external factors and navigating you through life's interactions. To work with your aura, you can try the following:

1. Visualize the sun's energy pouring over you.
2. Go outside and enjoy the sun.
3. Move your arms in a circulation motion in an outward direction as if you are trying to feel, explore, and dust the aura. It surrounds you. Reach for it.

YOUR AURA EXISTS
it is an energy field

it surrounds your body

it protects you

it sends energy out it filters energy in

Signs of an impacted Aura

feeling uneasy around others

afraid of experiences

Difficulty setting boundries

You absorb other's energies

Chapter 3

Your Hands

When I was a child, my father came to me and said, "Rub your hands together." I watched him do this for about a minute, and then he separated his hands slightly, palms still facing each other.

"Feel that?" he asked, as I tried it. I smiled at him, feeling the warmth between my hands.

"That is energy," he said.

The body is like a magnet. We don't often think of the body in this way, but quite simply, all the basic elements of the universe (that means us too) contain a certain numbers of protons and neutrons in cells; therefore, there is a constant tug between negative and positive charges. What we think is what we attract. Our hands are powerful healing tools that also contain chakras on the palms of them. They are energy transporters, and they can move energy.

Energy that is stuck in the body can cause disease. Use your hands to heal yourself and loved ones by placing them on their or your own chakras. To feel the magnetic pull coming from your hands, rub them together for ten seconds, and then slightly move your hands apart (less than an inch from each other). That is energy! Feel for yourself.

1. Press your thumb on the wrist crease of your other hand. Do this slowly and deeply, finding all the nooks and crannies of your wrists and hands. Feel the tissue and bones and then move out toward each finger, ending at the nails by your cuticles, pressing the corner of your cuticles. The benefit of doing this is so that you can begin to work with your own meridians. As mentioned, most meridians either end or start on your feet, hands, or face. Palpating, pressing, and/or rubbing these points will disperse blocked energy. Blocked energy will usually feel painful to touch. Do not shy away from it. Do not hurt yourself; find a comfortable and happy medium. Rub with the intention of dispersing blocked energy.

2. Do the same with your feet, starting at the ankles.

3. Make sugar scrubs using home ingredients and massage your hands and feet. You will need raw sugar, white sugar, olive or coconut oil, a large bowl, hot water, and a container for storage. Mix a cup of raw sugar and a cup of white sugar with half a cup of the warm water. The warm water helps to mix the sugars together. Add the oil to your liking. You can also add a few drops of essential oil to give it a nice smell. You can use any kind of oil. Avocado and almond oils are also good choices. You can store this in a container in the refrigerator for about two months.

4. Get creative and pamper yourself! Your feet carry you through life, and your hands help you do the things you love to do. They deserve some attention. Use the scrub to rub away blocked energy.

Energy usually becomes stuck in between joints. Applying pressure, massage, and/ or movement on or around joints will release blockages and allow for better flow and wellness. Don't forget the mind. Notice your thoughts. See how if you are constantly thinking about negative things, you attract precisely those things into your life. Life is a wonderful dance between you and your thoughts. Do everything possible to keep your thoughts happy.

Explanations about the body, health, and medical issues usually come to us in form of difficult medical jargon. For some, this difficulty is enough to make a person fully confide in others about their health. I am not saying not to go with conventional medicine when it comes to disease; however, I do believe that it is important to understand that we are our own best healers, that we know more than we think, and that just as we can manifest illness, we can bring forth wellness. Feelings can qualify as proof, though we've been taught to ignore them. Go with your gut and truly begin to listen to your body and your mind. Listen to the different patterns that come up. Does a thought create tension in some part of your body? If so, identify it but do not judge it, stretch it out, or write it down. Explore these other systems whenever you have a chance and notice if there is a difference in you after doing so. Remember, you are in nature's Maserati. Explore its great gadgets.

Chapter 4

Watch Your Thoughts

From the last chapter, you may have assumed that my father was a perfect role model for me, but he was not. The only thing he ever taught me was how to feel energy with my hands. I choose to keep that memory of him because this is best for me, for my health. Why choose thoughts that taunt us and make us miserable? A better story is that he did his job and ignited within me the start of what would eventually be my life's work. Of course, I was not always as reasonable with him or myself. It took a long time to get to that point but this is what the journey is about— overcoming and finding happiness in the now as well as letting go of the pain from the past and becoming strong enough to be happy today. Sometimes it is easier to stay sad and place blame on others. Don't do it anymore. Practice controlling your thoughts.

There are wars everywhere, and I am not only talking about the wars outside ourselves or in other parts of the world. I am talking about the wars that exist within our minds, the ones that some fight with every day in order to get by with ease. The wars that I speak of are brought upon by false teachings throughout our lives, experiences that we've had, and the expectations we have of others and ourselves. They become habitual negative thought patterns that are etched inside of us. I remember the time before I started watching my thoughts; it felt as if I was on autopilot, endlessly repeating the same bad thoughts and experiences.

We have heard millions of times in our lives that we are our own worst enemies, but how true a statement! We have two options in life: Torture ourselves to the max with our own maddening thoughts or love ourselves to the max with our own maddening thoughts.

Do everything possible to make your thoughts lighter, for we are energy, and so it follows that if our vessels are filled with heaviness, it will emanate heaviness upon the world. We can see proof of that today in the world by turning on the news or even stepping outside of our homes. Aggression seems to be taking life in our streets, on trains, and in store checkout lines.

I had the most curious experience once at a Bed Bath & Beyond checkout line. The guy in front of me was actually pissed off because management realized the line was very long and began to open more cashier lines. He stood firmly, protesting that the opening of more lines was making things much more confusing. I couldn't help but laugh a little and think, *This guy is hilarious. He will complain about anything.* Don't chime in; don't be that person. If possible, uplift that person. There are so many conflicts in the world, some bigger than others, but the idea is to do the best you can for yourself, for we cannot control others.

Make the mundane an opportunity to practice watching your thoughts. Do not get intimidated by the word *meditation.* You do not have to be a totally Zen hippie type to start. Make watching your thoughts an experience adaptable to your individual style. Start small and incorporate it into something that you already have to do, like washing the dishes or doing the laundry. For example, instead of dreading that pile of dishes, enjoy the warm water pouring over your hands as you scrub. Think about how nice it was to have a meal on them. Appreciate that you have dishes. When doing laundry, appreciate how great it is that we can wash with a machine. Fold deliberately and notice the fresh smells of the soap.

There is no smooth way of doing it. You have to decide that you want to start watching your thoughts and consciously do it. Make it a habit, like flossing your teeth or taking a shower. Consider it the most important aspect of grooming.

Watching your thoughts requires you to own up to your own BS, making peace with it and letting a thought go if it is damaging to you. It took a lot for me to say to myself, "I will no longer be a victim. I am not dumb. My thoughts are valid. I am no longer that scared and disappointed child. I am brave because I overcame, and what I went through is gone and has made me what I am today." Why hold on to bad memories? We hold on because we believe that the culmination of those experiences makes us who we are. They become our identity, and who we are is something we do not want to lose. We relentlessly hold on to these thoughts, even if the memory of them continues to hurt us. I promise that you will not lose who you are if you let them go. Instead, you will be an improved version of yourself.

We all have our own issues, our own taunting little background voices, and again, this is what I believe connects us as humans. Of course we have issues! Before conception, we were comprised of infinite free-flowing potential. In the womb, we are cradled inside of our mothers' "safeness," and then we are born to a world that is unknown. At birth, we feel total sensory overload. It is foreign and scary. Then we are bombarded by concepts, ideas, and thoughts that are not even our own and often not even true. Wouldn't it be wonderful if our kids were taught early on that their parents are not all-knowing? I would imagine a lot of pain would be spared. So it's okay to have issues, but it is not okay to live in the past and to continue torturing ourselves and others with them.

Identify if you can sense variation and rhythm in your thought patterns. One may sound like monkey chatter and the other a calmer, more relaxed one. I know that this sounds foreign to some. I speak as if we have more than one voice in our minds. But if you listen closely, you will find a dance between varieties of thinking patterns. There is the bass of the inner self and the percussion of the mind, and though they cannot exist without each other, it is of the utmost importance to find balance between the two. Make your thoughts an awesome melody. The mind is the practical one, the one that gets things done. It warns to proceed with caution. For example, it tells you that you cannot afford to quit your job yet. It tends to remember the past. It is quick to highlight all the possibilities and what to avoid. It reminds us that last time, this or that happened. These are all good things. You need the mind, but it cannot always be the boss. The sound of the inner self, your essence, or spirit is the one that gets excited about the possibilities, the one that imagines and knows who you are, the one that knows that things will work out, the one that wants to love. To clarify, when I speak of spirit, I speak of your essence, your joy, your love. I do not speak of religion, for religion has created barriers and hate between us. It has separated us instead of joined us. We are all human. Watch your thoughts and pay attention to where they come from, but do not judge yourself or give up on your process. I bet you can even find other voices in there, like the whiney inner child's voice. Pay attention to your inner dialogue—but don't judge it. Let the inner self be the boss sometimes. Mind and inner self or spirit need to be in sync, for the mind is simply a tool for what is the essence of you.

Chapter 5

There Is Perfection in Imperfection

There is perfection in imperfection! Striving for perfection can sometimes limit us or even discourage us from proceeding with an idea, thought, or action. Our minds can become caught up or fickle with the idea of perfection and then give up—or develop negative habitual thoughts that constantly keep us down. Sometimes the mirage of perfection is pure procrastination.

Why want perfection or to achieve something exactly as it was done before by predecessors? You will manifest the idea in your own individual style. You will get into that yoga pose in your own way at your own pace. You do not have to be a flexible fat-free yogi to get benefit from a yoga pose, no matter how much you have to adapt the pose to your needs. You do not have to be a monk in order to get hold of your thoughts for at least one minute a day. You do not have to be a professional dancer in order to get joy from a dance class.

Why want to achieve something exactly as we perceive perfection to be when this perception is in constant change and almost impossible to capture? It is a mirage. Everyone's version of perfection is different. What we should seek is the experience and the joy of following through with the idea, thought, or desire to do something—to see our versions of our ideas out in the world. Believe in yourself, have fun, and don't be so hard on yourself.

Working with the lower chakras (root, womb, and solar plexus) can help bring your creativity to the surface. A balanced root chakra will give you security and the urge to be who you want to be in the world. In addition, it will activate the upper chakras to ignite the creativity and sense of self needed in order to proceed and establish who you are in the world. Aside from the clearing techniques described earlier, any rolling of the hips and opening and closing of the inner and outer thighs (the adductor and abductor muscles) can assist in creating movement in these energies. In addition, focusing on the core and twisting the torso can help and can be done at home easily. You can also sit on a comfortable surface with your back straight. Close your eyes and imagine the lower chakras emanating color from you. Breathe by allowing your lower belly to expand, slowly lifting the energy up with your mind. If you are connected with the angels or fairies, you can ask them to help. Imagine them pouring warm healing water over you. Imagine their tiny silver buckets and their arms and hands as they pour.

Chapter 6

Yin and Yang

Yin and yang is a philosophical concept dating from the third century BCE. I came to learn more about this concept during my time in massage therapy school, in which we were taught both Eastern and Western approaches for treating the body. I automatically gravitated more toward Eastern modalities when helping my clients and have since then continued my studies in this area.

This Chinese philosophical concept has also become popular in our culture. Today one can see its symbol worn as tattoos or even in jewelry pieces. You will also see it as a logo for a variety of bodywork establishments. Yin and yang is a concept that explains the nature of energy in the body and out in the world. It is my hope that after this chapter, you can start to practice looking at all things, including your thoughts in terms of yin and yang.

In the East, the body is viewed and examined

as being in between heaven and earth, heaven being yang and earth being yin. If you're not into the whole heaven and earth thing, you can think of it in terms of polarity or North and South. In other words, the body's energy must be in balance. Yin and yang is a way of defining qi, or life energy, that which flows in all things. It is the chaos that brought forth life. To explain qi further, Chinese medicine explains it in terms of the five elements: earth, fire, water, wood, and metal. They are taking the macrocosm, in this case qi, explaining it in terms of two polar opposites and then filtering that into the microcosm by sorting it into elements.

Disease is viewed in terms of imbalance of qi (life energy) within the five elements. This makes sense, as in Chinese philosophy, they see things in terms of cycles, and we can all agree that all things have cycles: birth, life, and death. Seasons have cycles, stars, and illness; and relationships have cycles. Take the time to observe the cycles in all things. What attracted me to this way of perceiving the body was its simplicity. When there is too much energy in the body, there can be a disturbance, and it is the case if there is too little. Therefore, striving for balance and energetic flow within the elements will bring forth optimal health. Yin and yang represents this balance, and if you begin to explore various forms of energy work or exercises, you will find that the goal for all of them is to create this balance between the poles for yourself. You will also find that the actual exercises are similar to each other.

When I was in school, there was a clear distinction between how our Eastern and Western teachers talked about and taught us about the body. For example, in our anatomy, myology, palpation, and physiology classes, we first had to learn the language or terminology that is used in the health profession so that we can know where things are in the body. We learned about the body by looking at pictures, models, or cadavers, which were usually displayed in anatomical position. We have all seen this position, perhaps at a doctor or chiropractor's office or even in a massage therapist's office. The human body is portrayed erectly, with the arms hanging on the side, the face and palms facing forward. When studying and/or talking about the physical body or a specific body part, students and professionals use the following terms:

1. Anterior, meaning in front of the body
2. Posterior, meaning behind the body
3. Inferior, meaning below
4. Superior, meaning above
5. Lateral, meaning away from the midline
6. Medial, meaning toward the midline of the body
7. Proximal, meaning closer to the trunk or attachment point
8. Distal, meaning away from the trunk

Here is an example of the above used in a sentence. There are adhesions on the superior aspect of the ovaries. This means that the adhesions are above the ovaries. Of course, if you've ever had a medical issue or surgical procedure and glanced over the final medical records for it, you would find much more complicated sentences sprinkled with all of the above medical jargon and then some. To me, the entire ordeal is similar to ordering a Grande as opposed to a large coffee at Starbucks. In the end, even though ordering a Grande may sound more important, it is the same bitter-tasting substance.

In the East, anatomical position is different, and so is the professional's navigational system. The arms are above the head as opposed to hanging toward the side. They also illustrate and consider the fourteen energetic pathways or meridians that exist in the body. They study the body from a more animated perspective. They take mind, body, and spirit into account. They recognize that sometimes disease is related to some other more abstract or emotional issue. They attempt to understand the body by observing the living.

In Eastern medicine, there are yin parts of the body (soft sides of the limbs) versus yang parts (hairy parts of the limbs.) The front of the body is yin, while the back is yang. The easiest way to understand this concept is in terms of excess or deficiency—or opposites. The front of the body is yin because it is the softer side of you, the part that contains all your important organs. The back is yang because it is harder, maybe even the tougher side of you. Organs are also either yin or yang, as are the flows of each meridian. Each organ belongs to a certain element.

Yin Organs

These include the liver, heart, pericardium, spleen, lung, kidneys, and Conception Vessel. Yin organs flow from Earth to heaven or from the feet to the head. What does that mean? Well, it simply means that the start of or the energetic flow of a particular yin meridian will always be from Earth (feet) to heaven (face).

Yang Organs

These include the gallbladder, small intestine, triple warmer, stomach, large intestine, bladder, and Governing Vessel. The start of the yang organs will always be from heaven (face) to earth (feet.)

Yin energy is softer, while yang is a little tougher. Yin is more inward, while yang is more outward. Yin is quiet; yang is louder. Try to identify what yin and yang are in your everyday life. For example, I'll start you off. Morning is yang, and nighttime is yin. Being happy is yang, and being sad is yin. Wanting to go out dancing is yang, while wanting to stay in with a book is yin. Mind is yang, and spirt is yin. When you start looking at all aspects of life in this way, you can then start to strive for balance; wellness will eventually follow.

Balancing between Yin and Yang Energy

There are many exercises and practices such as qigong and tai chi that are centered on balancing the self between heaven and earth. Tai chi is a form of meditation in motion practiced in Chinese traditions, and qigong is a form of health system integrating breath, intention, and postures meant to align life force energy. In qigong, for example, they work mostly with Conception and Governing Vessel. To reiterate, both Conception and Governing Vessels are meridians. Conception governs all your yin meridians and Governing Vessel all your yang meridians. They are important because they play vital roles in circulating qi (life energy) in your body's energetic pathways.

Simply, what you want to do is find a time a day when it is quiet. Usually mornings are best so that you can have a fresh start to your day. Stand straight. You can do this in front of mirror if it is not distracting. Find what works for you. Everyone is different. Bend your knees slightly and tuck in your tailbone. Make sure to relax your glute muscles. Your back should be straight, your tongue touching the back of your upper teeth, your head slightly tucked. Your feet should be firmly planted on the floor. I find that not wearing shoes feels more grounding. Bend over as far as you can toward your feet and scoop up yin energy all the way up, lifting your arms over to grab yang energy, then pour it over yourself. You can do this three times.

If you prefer visualization techniques, you may hold the same stance as described and imagine that your feet are sinking into the earth like roots and that yin energy is lifting up from the roots, up to your legs. You can imagine a ray of sun shining down, feeling the warmth embracing you with yang energy. The most important thing is that you do not obsess about following my instructions or any instructions exactly when doing this. Find your own way. There is no way of doing anything wrong. You have the gist of it, so just balance between heaven and Earth or North and South.

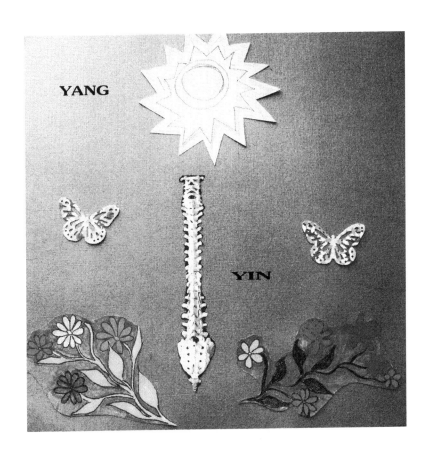

Chapter 7

Elements and Energy

If you pay attention, you will see that everything in nature has a rhythm, a certain flow. What most attracted me to Eastern approaches for health and wellness is that when a practitioner assesses a client, he or she listens to the sound of the client's voice, notices any smells, looks at the health of the skin, touches, and asks questions about the client's life. I love that they recognize that health is about the mind, body, and spirit connection. When they question, they are listening for any signs of imbalance within the individual's energy. They are making sure that qi (life energy) is flowing. They are thinking about five elements as they do this: fire, earth, metal, water, and wood. These elements are how they can recognize energy, identify where the issue is, and determine if it is kyo (deficient) or jitsu (excessive). Each element has an associated yin and yang organ and therefore its associated meridians.

If you've ever been to an acupuncturist or energy worker, you may know that he or she will feel for a pulse, look at your tongue, or feel around on your *hara* (your belly) to obtain information. When feeling your pulse, the person is listening for energy patterns within the meridians. The tongue is looked at to determine any discoloration, shape, and coating that can lead to clues about the client's condition within his or her energetic system. The hara (again, the abdominal area) is also a diagnostic tool because there are areas that pertain to specific organs on it. All of these are diagnostic tools, and what they are listening or feeling for is excess or deficiently within a specific meridian. Practitioners will also ask many questions in order to make sure that they can pinpoint where the imbalance is.

Each of us has all aspects of the elements in our physical and emotional makeup, but usually one or two elements predominate over the others, depending on the individual. Each element has distinct characteristics and is associated with yin and yang meridians. Remember, meridians are energy channels that exist in the body. They have distinct unchanging pathways, and each pertains to an organ. When a meridian is out of balance, it can cause disease, pain, or mental anguish. I've said this before, but I think it is important to reiterate that the reason yoga, bodywork, acupuncture, and other forms of energy work can be beneficial is because they are directly working with the meridian energy channels by either stretching the meridian to promote energetic flow or sticking a needle on the point to disperse blocked energy. Think of a highway in a traffic jam. An accident causes all other cars to stop or move slowly. It is the same with a blockage in a meridian channel. If there is a block, then energy cannot flow to where it should be going, disrupting all other channels and manifesting as discomfort, pain, or disease. Just as a meridian can be flowing too slowly, it can also be moving too quickly, which is not an ideal situation either.

To go back to the characteristics of the elements, each element has a time of day. This does not mean it stops at other times, only that the energy for that particular meridian tends to be stronger during particular times. In addition, they have a particular taste that is associated with them, as well as smell, season, color, climate, and emotion. When looking at the elements, make sure you are honest with yourself. We all have each of the elements. The key here is to take the information about the elements, identifying your individual issues and where they fall so that you can work with those elements on your own. Also remember that humans are complex. Take everything with a grain of salt; trust your inner healer.

Earth

Earth's season is Indian summer. It is a singing sweet energy that cares about others; it is balanced and strong. The organs that are associated with earth are stomach, from 7 a.m. to 9 a.m., and spleen, from 9 a.m. to 11 a.m. The emotion of Earth is worry because it genuinely cares about others. Stomach is associated with transformation and transportation, while spleen filters blood. General signs of imbalance can include weight fluctuation, circulation problems, and irregular eating habits. When thinking about Earth energy and its associated organs, think about what it means to be the stomach. The stomach is a muscular organ that is in charge of capturing the food you give it, breaking them down, and sending it to the small intestine, which is a fire organ. The nature of Earth energy is to distribute and transport for transformation. We don't often think of our organs as extensions of us, but they are the micro and we are the macro. We also don't think of our organs as having a *nature*, but they do. The spleen, which is anatomically next to the stomach, filters blood to support your immune system. Its energy is also in the business of protecting you. An Earth type of person, like the stomach and spleen, is a giver, caring and protecting.

Unbalanced Earth energy can cause an individual to care too much about others and become intrusively caring, sometimes even being passive-aggressive with others if they feel their *giving* is not accepted or wanted. If you tend to be stuck in Earth imbalance, I find that it is best to focus the caring on yourself. People who tend to be Earth types are down-to-earth, caring, adaptable to others, reliable, and territorial. While some of these characteristics are wonderful to have, it is important to understand that balance in all things is everything. There is such a thing as caring too much, especially if it is starting to affect your health. If you are constantly adapting to the needs of others, for example, this will eventually play its course and cause that Earth type to become upset and then passive-aggressive. Understand that you do not have to be an Earth type to have an Earth imbalance. For example, a person who is more of a metal type can suffer from indigestion if something is going on with someone he or she cares about. Again, I can't stress this idea enough: we all have a bit of all the elements in us. What is important is to begin to start paying attention to yourself. Start by identifying what element feels familiar to you.

How to support Earth

Do this by rolling the ankles, elevating the legs, and stretching the quads. Dancing the Twist can be good, as the action of slightly squatting and twisting the hips and waist can assist in bringing spleen energy up. Twisting your abs and arching your lower back so that your belly can pop out is also a great stomach energy supporter. Also, when making deep belly sounds with your mouth, feel how your voice can come from deep within the bottom of your gut. Earth is also very much connected to root chakra.

The following position is a good Earth stretch:

Fire

If humans had wings, would they be made out of cartilage? I've always asked myself this question. I imagine that if humans did have wings, they would probably originate from somewhere in the lower back, extending diagonally toward the scapula and ending at the deltoid. Perhaps the actual wings would be made of cartilage, a firm and flexible type of connective tissue. The scapula is a winglike-looking structure. Embracing the scapula in a triangular motion and extending toward the face flows small intestine energy (small intestine meridian), and beneath that, starting at the armpit, we can find heart energy (heart meridian).

The small intestine and heart are related to the element of fire and the season of summer. Fire is about being delighted for life. It is energy that sparks the desire of wanting to fly. Fire energy helps us to interpret the world. Fire is our *shen*, our presence in the world. Think of a fully blossomed flower in the summer. Think of its presence. This is fire. Think of a butterfly and its wings fluttering with excitement. This is fire energy. I always feel that I can activate fire energy by rolling my shoulders and pretending that I have wings.

The small intestine is responsible for dividing the pure from the impure within the body but also outside the body. It monitors what people, events, situations, and external forces are pure or impure (healthy) for us. Heart is the pump for the soul, responsible for circulation and connection.

Heart energy is most active between 11 a.m. and 1 p.m., while small intestine energy is most active between 1 p.m. and 3 p.m. This does not mean that the energy stops during other times in the day. This means that during these times, the energy is at its best. It gives us clues. For example, if you are not at your best during a certain meridian's peak time, then that can mean something is off balance within that element. The emotion of fire is joy.

Typical fire imbalance can present as having pain in the shoulders, feeling bloated, having hot or cold food cravings, feeling sadness that affects your ability to focus, experiencing difficulty weighing out options, feeling chest pains, having constant on-the-go behavior, being prone to excess, and craving bitter tastes.

Pericardium (yin) and triple warmer (yang) are also fire meridians. Fire is the only element that contains four meridians. Pericardium, a membranous sac enclosing the heart, assists in regulating energy flow inside and around the heart. It protects you by defusing or redirecting excessive energy caused by emotional pain, illness, and general overactivity. Triple warmer goes by many names. You may see it as triple energizer or triple burner. TW is not an organ; it is actually a collection of metabolic centers, which also includes organs. The purpose of the TW is to maintain balance within the lymphatic and immune systems in your body.

How to support fire

When I was studying shiatsu years ago, I learned the "cleaning the wings" technique for working with fire energy. During this technique, the bodyworker applies touch and/or provides movement in the areas surrounding the shoulders and scapula. You can do this yourself by rolling your shoulders, neck, and wrists while raising your arms. Pretending to shoot a bow and arrow is also good for fire energy. In addition, you can use a yoga block to clean your own wings. Place the block on the floor and lie down on the block, making sure the edges of the block are meeting the edge of the scapula. You can also find other areas to massage by lying down on the block, allowing your weight to sink in where the pressure feels good. For example, the block is placed horizontally between your shoulder blades. By rolling your shoulders while in this position, you are applying self-massage between the scapulae. In addition, by allowing your head to drop back while resting on the block, you will be able to massage the base of your skull with the edge of the block by gently moving your head from side to side and front to back.

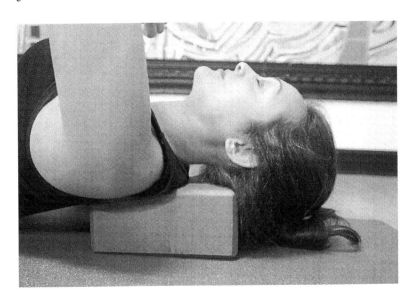

Fire Stretches:

Water

When I think of water, I think of purification and going with the flow of one's environment. Water goes with the flow and is introspective. A water type of person can be curious but cautious, insightful, and sensitive. Water, according to five-element theory, pertains to the season of winter. Its emotion is fear, and it is associated with bladder and kidney meridians. The kidney is the holder of your *jing*, your essence or template, while bladder is the receiver and purifier of things given to it by the small intestine. The bladder meridian is long, starting at the inner canthus of the eyes, extending over the head and straight down the back parallel to the spine, making a sort of loop on the gluteus maximus and again going straight down the leg. Kidney starts at the ball of the foot, looping around the ankles and flowing upward on the inside (or yin side) of the legs. Bladder time is from 3 p.m. to 5 p.m., while kidney time is from 5 p.m. to 7 p.m. Some symptoms of unbalanced water energy can present as backaches, sciatica, weakness in the knees, arthritis, impotence, low sex drive, and being fearful of life experience. It can also present as urinary tract infections and frequent urination.

Working with Water Meridians

Because bladder meridian is hugging the head and spine, I find that running your fingers through your hair and head with medium pressure can be helpful in activating this meridian. Gallbladder meridian is also around the head, but I will talk about that next. After running your fingers through your hair and head a couple of times, start to explore the base of your skull with your fingers and palms, moving down your neck and then clasping your shoulders. Stretch your back by trying to touch your toes. If you can't reach, that's okay; little by little, your flexibility will improve. Flex your feet and then point your toes. You can roll a tennis ball on the ball of your foot to activate kidney energy.

Because the bladder meridian flows through the erector muscles and hamstrings, you want to make sure your legs and back remain as straight as possible. It is okay to bend your legs if your hamstrings are too tight. You can bend your knees and back to slightly release any pain, trying to keep your legs and back as straight as possible.

The following pose opens the kidney meridian:

Metal

Metal is that meticulous energy that finds beauty in perfection. It is associated with the season of autumn and with the emotion of grief. If hindered, it can cause difficulties with letting go of objects, emotions, ideas, or memories. I always believed that trees have the oldest of souls. They are the perfect examples of how we should live. They stand patiently and calmly, their branches dancing with the wind. They allow their leaves to fall, knowing that they will soon be back again. When metal meridians are not flowing freely on their skin-deep pathways, people can tend to hold on to things that no longer serve them. Metal is where the *po* is stored. According to Chinese medicine, *po* is the corporal self, the self that goes away with death. It is the area between spirt and reality, and it keeps us in the present moment, sifting through what is essential and letting go of experiences that no longer serve us. The organs/meridians associated with metal are lung, which is yin, and large intestine, which is yang. The lungs are in charge of bringing air into the body so that it can refresh all its organs and systems, while the large intestine helps to eliminate and make space for today. Metal is the wonderful tug between bringing in and letting go. Lung is most active between 3 a.m. and 5 a.m., while large intestine energy is most active between 5 a.m. and 7 a.m. Signs of general imbalance in the metal element are seen in the health of the skin. One can suffer from dry skin, acne, and/

or other skin manifestations. Any issues with the lungs such as sinus problems, bronchitis, asthma, and pneumonia can point to a metal imbalance as well as bowel irregularities such as constipation. On a more emotional aspect, an imbalance can also appear as an excess of grief or sadness or being detached, self-righteous, or too proud. Metal can also have difficulties with letting go or wanting to keep things perfectly traditional or resistant to change. People who tend to be metal energies can be meticulous, organized, rational, and disciplined individuals.

Working with Metal Meridians

Do chest-opening stretches, being mindful of the breath and rolling the neck. Remember, breathing in itself can be an entire meditation if you focus your attention as follows: explore taking breaths with the nose, feeling if your neck muscles are assisting with breathing. If so, try to take a breath without using the neck. Instead focus on taking it by elevating the ribs. Feel how your ribs lift and how your belly fills up. A tai chi practice would be excellent to support metal energy, and it would be something that a metal energy can understand because of its elegant and precise nature. Tai chi can be described as a form of meditation combined with movement. Shooting an imaginary bow and arrow slowly, alternating between left and right sides of the body, is one of the poses in tai chi. The action of opening the chest and arm directly opens the lung and stretches the large intestine meridians. In this pose, you are also opening other meridians like triple warmer, pericardium, and heart. For me, what is most important is for people to find the form of energy work that is best for them. Equally as important is to find a way to do these yourself in the comfort of your home. Even five minutes a day will make a difference.

The following pose supports
Metal meridians:

Wood

Wood energy is determination, ambitious, and decisiveness. It is bold, and it initiates action. It has to be because the organs associated with wood are gallbladder, from 11 p.m. to 1 a.m. (yang), and liver (yin), from 1 a.m. to 3 a.m. Think of the nature of the liver and gallbladder. The liver has a serious job to do for you and has no time to waste. The liver is a blood filer, it is a metabolizer of nutrients, it detoxifies substances that are harmful, and it makes blood-clotting proteins. The gallbladder is responsible for storing and producing the sending of bile. They do not have time to be introspective and curious like the water element. They do not have time to worry like the Earth element; they have to decide quickly for the protection of you! Think of a large tree determined to move up higher and stronger than all the other trees. This is the feeling of wood energy. The emotion associated with wood is anger, and its season is spring. An example of wood energy is when an individual feels determined and works hard toward the goal.

Wood out of balance can manifest as pain in

the muscles, tendons, and ligaments. You can also get clues about the wood element imbalance by looking at the health of the eyes and nails. Headaches and menstrual pain can also point to wood imbalance. We've all encountered wood energy in our lives. Its voice is bold and direct. A wood type can also be prone to mood swings, become frustrated, or have angry outbursts when out of balance.

Working with Wood Meridians

Any side stretches of the upper body and lower body will support the gallbladder meridian. The liver meridian starts from the outside or lateral corner of the big toe, up via the inner thighs, farther still toward the rib, and ending below the nipple. Any stretching of the inner thighs, movement of the ankles, and stretching of the sides of your core and extremities will activate movement within the wood element.

So now that you have the overview of all the elements, you can identify where your imbalance is and work directly with that element or work by using either the control cycle or the mother-child cycle. Five-element theory is based on the idea that if an element is out of balance, it will disrupt all other elements, and as I've mentioned before, each element is associated with an organ. So in the mother-child cycle, fire is the mother of Earth, Earth of metal, metal of water, water of wood, and wood of fire. This means the mother feeds the child. If the mother element is out of balance, then the child can be impacted, creating imbalance in the entire cycle. In the control cycle, fire melts metal, earth stops water, metal cuts wood, and wood controls earth.

Five-element control and mother-child cycle:

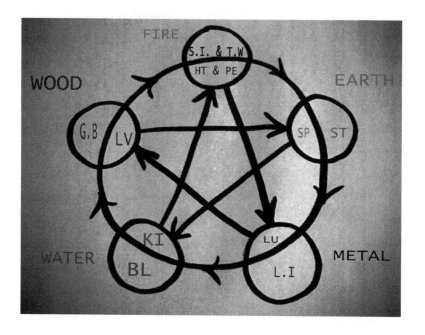

SI (Fire)	Small intestine	Yang	1 p.m. to 3 p.m.
TW (Fire)	Triple warmer	Yang	9 p.m. to 11 p.m.
HT (Fire)	Heart	Yin	11 a.m. to 1 p.m.
PE (Fire)	Pericardium	Yin	7 p.m. to 9 p.m.
ST (Earth)	Stomach	Yang	7 a.m. to 9 a.m.
SP (Earth)	Spleen	Yin	9 a.m. to 11 a.m.
L.I (Metal)	Large intestine	Yang	5 a.m. to 7 a.m.
LU (Metal)	Lung	Yin	3 a.m. to 5 a.m.

BL (Water)	Bladder	Yang	3 p.m. to 5 p.m.
KI (Water)	Kidney	Yin	5 p.m. to 7 p.m.
GB (Wood)	Gallbladder	Yang	11 p.m. to 1 a.m.
LV (Wood)	Liver	Yin	1 a.m. to 3 a.m.

Example: If you are experiencing symptoms in the Earth element, you can work with wood because wood controls Earth—or you can work with the fire element because fire is the mother of Earth. Refer to the sections above about working with wood meridian or whatever meridian you need to work with.

Thinking of conditions in terms of excess or deficiency:

The beauty of five-element theory is that once you figure out what is out of balance, you can work with the meridian in order to get the balance needed for improved health. So take, for example, feelings of restlessness, frustration, and agitation. Would you consider these to feel like conditions of excess or deficient energy? Compare them with feelings of pensiveness or weepiness. How do they feel for you in your body? Examine the feelings of weakness versus stiffness. Does your pain feel more sharp than dull? Be mindful of your pain and try to describe how it feels in your body. It is similar to thinking of things in terms of yin and yang, as I've described in the prior chapter.

A good way of gauging and starting deeper work with the meridians is as follows:

Remember those extra meridians I spoke about earlier? To refresh, there are fourteen meridians, twelve pertaining to organs, and two are called Central and Governing Vessels. Meridians have their own specific flow, and they run on the surface of the skin. The Governing Vessel is in charge of all yang meridians, including replenishing spinal fluids, keeping your mind and body vibrant. It shoots up straight from the base of the spine (tailbone) to the top of the head and then around between the eyebrows, ending at the top of the lip. Remember, this space between the eyebrows is also the third eye chakra center, responsible for intuition and integration of thoughts. Conception Vessel is in charge of all the yin meridians. It runs straight up the front of the body from the perineum (area between the anus and scrotum or vulva) and through the throat chakra, connecting in the mouth with the Governing Vessel at the bottom of the lip. Both GV and CV supply energy to all the other meridians. Working with these two meridians will nourish all the other meridians. Activating the orbit, a.k.a. the microcosmic orbit, means allowing these two energies to complete a figure eight–shaped circuit between the Conception Vessel and Governing Vessel.

Activating the Orbit

Stand straight or sit, if possible in front of a mirror. Make sure that your chest is up and that you are not slouching. Tighten the area below the belly button, or womb chakra by pushing in towards the spine and up towards the ribs. Now relax the glutes and focus on the perineum (area between the anus and scrotum or vulva).

Visualize a white stream of light flowing up from this space. Watch it flow straight up, passing your belly button and sternum (area between your breasts), passing your throat chakra to the bottom of the lips. Watch the white stream of light lock at the button of the lip and then disappear to the tailbone. From the tailbone, move the white stream up straight through the spine. Feel the replenishing of the spine as it moves up through the neck and around the head, ending at the top of the lip. Continue to visualize the orbit, feeling free to change the color of the stream as you wish. Remember, there is perfection in imperfection. Create your own orbit. Get familiar with the concept of it and find your own way to do this. There is no way of getting it wrong.

Chapter 8

Finding Your Center

Throughout the years, as I continued my education and career in energy science and bodywork, I've learned that the concept of finding your center is not always clear for others. It is not always the norm to raise your hand in a yoga class or interrupt meditation hour to ask, "What the heck does that mean? When did I lose my center? Am I unbalanced or flawed? Where exactly is my center? I didn't even know I needed it!"

The mind may continue to ask taunting questions in this way throughout an entire class or session, discouraging you or blurring the reasons you attended the class in the first place. If you focus and go back to the reason you took the class in the first place, you will understand the center and then begin to find it more often.

To say it simply, finding your center is a delicate state of being in which an individual finds balance and integration between mind, body, and spirit. I would like to clarify that whenever I talk of the spirit, I am not talking about dogma. I always use *spirit* in the sense of one's individual consciousness, the wonderful you that is here in the present, the one who has sorted through different concepts of existence throughout the years and has come up with your own conclusions. Always respect the collective you.

How do we begin?

Be the CEO of your thoughts – I think that everyone can agree that the mind is complex. To delve into its complexity would take forever, so to get to your center as quickly as possible, I'd like to invite you to begin to observe your thoughts. Do not judge your thoughts; simply notice them. Notice how a particular thought makes you feel. With some time and practice, you will find that some thoughts are not worth having around because they torture you. For example, if you have consistent thoughts about how you are not good enough or smart enough, notice how you feel after the thought. Do you feel fearful? Angry? Notice the feeling and try to identify where it came from. What early life event started this pattern of thinking? It is difficult to do, but realize that it no longer serves you. Understand that it is not true. The more you sort through your negative thoughts, the closer you will get to your center. Your centered self does not want to be sad. It wants to be happy. The better you get at firing these thoughts, the closer you will get to your center.

Breathe – Without breath, there is no life! Take deep breaths. Do not be cheap with the air you breathe. Make it a point to breathe. Fill your nose with air; allow the ribs to expand and lift, your belly filling it with air. Always breathe with intention. For me, setting aside time to lie on the bed or floor alone, paying attention to the breath and/or the body's intricate little corners, has always taken me straight to my center. The body is a magical vehicle. Notice it! Acknowledge that there is blood flowing through your veins.

Techniques

1. While breathing with intention, place the palm of your hand between your eyebrows. Place your other palm about one inch

above or below the belly button. Hold until you feel a sense of peace.

2. Spend time alone in nature and watch its effortlessness. For example, I always love to watch the flow of a river.

3. Write down the thoughts that do not make you feel good and throw them away. For example, I will write down a thought and then burn the paper over the toilet and watch it flush away.

4. Label your breathing. For example, as you inhale, say to yourself, "receive." As you exhale say, "let go."

Remember that finding your center is a personal journey and practice. Get creative and have fun with it. Only you will know where and what your center is. There is a delicate dance between mind, body, and spirit; and it will always feel amazingly light and refreshing. Pay attention to how you feel. That will be your compass.

Chapter 9

Of Spirit and Things

In my practice and throughout life in general, it was troubling for me to continue hearing the words "I'm not able to tap into my soul." It was troubling because, for me, there has always been a distinct difference between my soul's presence and the chatter coming from my brain. I wanted to illustrate this difference for those who couldn't. Difficult task. I learned to do my best for those who wanted to tap into it.

As time passed, I found it curious that for some reason, men tended to be the ones with the most difficulty. I would like to clarify and say that from experience, I do know that this is not the case for all men and have encountered women with the same dilemma. It is worth saying, however, that men have constantly been deprived of such connections, at times from the very women that have raised them. In a patriarchal world, where men are expected to be powerful, I suppose the soul has no purpose.

The monkey brain wins! In the same manner, throughout history women have been labeled as too sensitive, unstable, and more "spiritual." These are extremes. Female and male concepts are representations. They are the yin and the yang. They cannot exist without each other. Luckily, times have been changing. I love that the word *manny* is now a thing, that women are showing their *yanger* sides.

In order to connect with your spirit, you must want to do the work. Often this means watching the self under monkey chatter control. What I mean by monkey chatter is the streamline of thoughts that are fear-based or negative. You will find that many of these thoughts are not true. They have been derived by some event that was not under your control. If you start paying attention to these thoughts objectively during the day and work through them, you will begin to sort them out and identify what early life events have caused them. Do not judge these thoughts or events; just notice, identify, and let them go, for they no longer serve you in the present. I understand that letting things go is no easy task. That is easier said than done, but to this my answer is that one must have the urge to be happy. Quite simply one cannot be happy if you don't consciously make the effort to let painful events and memories go. Remember, the ego wants to keep these in your memory bank because it has recognized pain as part of its identity. Do not let your pain be your identity.

Cardio exercise is a great way to tire out the ego. Intend to tire out your ego. Do not only go through the motions of getting to the gym or working out on your home treadmill. Right after exercising, lie down, close your eyes, and place your hand on your heart. Feel the thumps. Feel the blood flowing. This is spirit, for it is encased in your body. Mind and body is a tool for your spirit. It is the vehicle. You are not your negative experiences.

Never underestimate the power of gratitude, and trust me that I know it is sometimes difficult to find gratitude, especially if you are living an unwanted situation. Despite your current circumstances, I am sure you can find things to be grateful about. Make a list of them and read them to yourself when you are feeling bad. I usually read my list early in the morning or before bed. The list must name things that you are actually grateful about. It can be as simple as having chocolate brownies on the list. The idea is that it must be honest. The universe knows when you are lying or simply going through the motions.

Another quick route to spirit is through laugher, play, dance, music, and imagination. Watch something funny on television or watch a good animated film. Play music and dance by yourself. Use your imagination to locate events that have brought you joy and choose to keep those in your mind as you go about your day.

Chapter 10

Tame the Tenacious Inner Child

The inner child is something you may have heard or read about throughout the years. You may have also heard that ignoring the inner child can somehow poke a few splinters onto our present lives if we don't tend to it. These "splinters" can manifest as physical pain, illness, or general feelings of sadness.

So what is the inner child and why does it need taming? The inner child is the self of the past, the one that continues to hold on to thoughts that no longer serve a purpose in the present. These thoughts create feelings that are heavy and do not allow us to move on. We hear the thought's bratty little voice in our minds, whining and blaming others for pain that was perceived long ago. By doing this, we relive the pain repeatedly in the present.

Working with the inner child is extremely difficult because it requires us to be brave when looking back objectively at our childhoods. There are loads of sensitive topics and feelings around it, so we avoid it and leave it there to fester. I find that by noticing the beauty of childhood, one can begin to start to want to work with the inner child. Locate the point in time when you were at ease. Then notice the contrasts, the pain, disappointment, joys, fears, love, embarrassment, and confusion. Recognize that every human in the world has experienced these feelings in their childhoods at some point. You are not alone. Accept that we are all humans, especially your caregivers, lovers, husbands, wives, friends, bosses. Let go and forgive yourself and others.

Tending to the inner child requires us to be open-minded and accept that there is a self of the past that needs grooming and that we need to be ruthlessly practical about when, how often, and what we do consistently for the inner child. Remember, in this moment you have control over your perception on a particular painful childhood experience.

Tending to Your Inner Child

1. Do not ignore the inner child, for he or she will become even more pestilent.

2. Make a pact with yourself that you will only tend to your inner child every day for at least ten minutes. Do not baby it by always catering to it.

3. When you have time, close your eyes, visualizing the self of the past and the self of the present. Embrace each other and say, "I love you and understand your pain. I am stronger today because of you. I am releasing the pain and forgiving myself and others for it." A quicker way of doing this is to draw the infinity symbol between you and your inner child.

4. Do not beat yourself up if you break the pact. Every day is blank. Try again.

5. Make it a point to clear your thoughts when you wake up. Find something that you are truly grateful for. Yes, even chocolate, beer, or anything else you enjoy. It can be anything, as long as you are truly grateful about the thought you choose to focus on.

Do not just go through the motions of your morning routine.

6. Reward yourself! Buy yourself flowers, candy, or whatever makes you happy!

7. Find the time to do the things you love to do.

I know that working with the inner child may sound difficult, especially if you focus on the disappointments of childhood. Try thinking about the joys of childhood instead. Think about the things that were fun—the laughs and the excitement—and then be ruthlessly practical. If a thought comes up that disrupts your present ease, say goodbye with forgiveness, understanding, and respect for the self of the past.

Chapter 11

Visualization

I cannot stress the importance of visualization enough; however, I do understand that it can be difficult. I know this from personal experience, from facing my own mental barriers and emotional issues from the past. All I want to say about it is that with dedication, imagination, and the urge to overcome your personal issues, it will become second nature. You will become a master of knowing your thoughts. You will understand where they came from. Once you know that, you will stop them from ruling over your life.

Visualization is effective because you can start to repattern your negative thoughts. We all have things to overcome. My *things* may be different from yours, but they are not more or less painful. Understanding that fact is so important because it reminds us that we are all humans and that we are not alone in the world with our pain. Truly knowing that you are not alone can help.

Not pretending to be perfect is key, accepting yourself and the people around you as human beings, understanding that it truly does matter what we think and how we feel. It matters to your health and to the world. We are so much more alike than we believe we are. We are more than the roles we play in the world—more than the bills we have to pay or the "mistakes" we've made.

In my work, I've seen many examples of pain or illness manifested because of more complex life issues originating from childhood or early adolescence. For example, a woman who had been molested manifested her pain as issues with her reproductive organs. A man who used to be artistic lost his abilities after his father's death. In a lot of ways, even as adults, I've learned that we are still like children. This is because our spirits always remains pure. It is the body that ages. We must be diligent with our thought processes and abilities to let go. Love yourself. Reliving negative experiences in your thoughts is not loving yourself. Do your best and don't give up.

Take the time to imagine. Remember when we were kids and how we used to use our imaginations? Visualization is the same. Instead of choosing to think about things that feel bad, why not think about the things that feel good, like imagining ourselves in a place that we would love, surrounded by delicious goodies. You might ask what the point of this is. The point is that what we feel we attract and what sparks a feeling is a thought.

Chapter 12

Get Silly, for the Journey Is Infinite

Why are adults so serious, so quick to turn down new ideas or even have fun? Where is the lightness? Why do we always have to make things so heavy and complicated? Why do we have such a hard time letting go of ideas and concepts that no longer serve us as individuals and as a race? There are so many emotional and social answers to those questions, but trust me that pinballing them back and forth will not give us the answer or get us to happiness. You are the only one who can get yourself to happiness, so stop the insanity and get silly, for this journey is infinite.

Our journey is a beautiful and infinite one, expansive in nature. Everything that you experienced, good and bad, I can assure you taught you a lesson and made you grow. Heal yourself, for we are magical beings. Take notice of the beauty that surrounds us, including the bodies that carry and sustain us.

The feeling of having innocent fun or doing something silly syncs us to the inner being, to the magic that is our existence. I believe it is the quickest and most direct route to the spirit. Look at children and animals and learn from them. We often don't believe they can teach us, but they can. I am grateful to have very vivid memories of my childhood. Some of the things that I recall have served as proof of the wisdom children have. One in particular has given me strength throughout the years. When I was nine years old, I was diagnosed with ITP, as mentioned, which meant that I had a low platelet count in my blood. I was sick for about a year, having to go for weekly blood work and transfusions in the hematology department at Mount Sinai Hospital. There I would see kids with all kinds of blood disorders, but most vivid in my mind were the kids with leukemia. I remember their smiles underneath bald heads as the clowns came to play and do artwork with us. Mostly I remember the day I returned from my surgery. Because of the ITP, I had to have a splenectomy. They had placed my bed next to a girl with leukemia. At the time, I didn't really understand what leukemia was. As I was placed next to her and crying from the pain coming from my fresh incision, she came over to me and stroked my hair. She brought me ice chips and told me that everything would be okay. Her voice was soft but knowing. At the time, I didn't recognize this act as something beautiful. I was young and struggling with my own pain, but years later, as I thought about it without even knowing if she had survived, it was one of the most inspiriting experiences of my life. Despite her disease being much more severe than mine was, this little girl found the strength to console me. This memory still brings me inspirational tears.

At times, we can become caught up in our own mental barriers, in our own pain. We can often be too proud to say, "I was wrong." Too scared to say, "I love you." Too rigid to try new things. As we navigate the universe, always know that things are not always as they appear. As humans, we are masters at wearing our social masks. Remembering that our fellow humans can be going through something on the inside is important, that they are perhaps as scared or insecure as you are. Be kind to others, for everyone has his or her own internal battles.

Paola Collazos, LMT

Follow your heart and know that feelings do qualify as proof. They are your compass and can tell you when to stay away or proceed. Everything is vibration. Nothing matters other than your perception.

Afterword

At the time of conception, we are infinite potential. We are energy incased in skin—human form.

At birth, we are still infinite potential, but we are bombarded with sensory overload.

Think about it ...

We are ripped away from one state of being into a completely different environment and form.

There is now cold, light, and sounds to process and deal with. There are concepts, emotions, people, and circumstances that shape us.

Time and experience makes us forget that we come from that same magic that we are always trying to define as all-knowing and all-powerful! But the truth is that we are all-knowing and all-powerful. Children and animals still remember this. Get silly, for the journey is infinite.

About the Author

Paola Collazos is a Reiki master, energy medicine practitioner, and a licensed massage therapist. She discovered her calling as a bodyworker while searching for ways to heal herself. Enamored by philosophy, metaphysics, and spiritual teachings, Paola still affirms that nothing has enlightened her more than studying human anatomy and physiology, its subtle rhythms and its physical and mental manifestations. She continues to be inspired by an individual's ability to heal oneself. She has been working with people from all lifestyles since 2002. She is an artist, poet, teacher, and writer who has uniquely integrated all her skills in order to promote peace and enlightenment by helping others heal themselves.

Made in the USA
Middletown, DE
06 January 2018